Henry Ford: 1863 – 1947

"I will build a motor car for the great multitude. It will be large enough for the family but small enough for the individual to run and care for. It will be constructed of the best materials, by the best men to be hired, after the simplest designs that modern engineering can devise. But it will be so low in price that no man making a good salary will be unable to own one – and enjoy with his family the blessing of hours of pleasure in God's great open spaces."

FORD
MODEL T
Michael Allen

CONTENTS

Foulis

Haynes

A FOULIS Motoring Book

First published 1987

© Haynes Publishing Group

Published by:

Haynes Publishing Group,
Sparkford, Near Yeovil,
Somerset BA22 7JJ

Haynes Publications Inc.
861 Lawrence Drive, Newbury
Park, California 91320, USA

**British Library Cataloguing in
Publication Data**

Allen, Michael, 1939 Mar. 11 –
Model T Ford super profile. – (Super
profile series)
1. Ford Model T automobile
I. Title II. Series
629.2'222   TL215.F7

ISBN 0-85429-587-9

**Library of Congress catalog
card number** 86-83365

Editor: Judith St. Clair-Pedroza
Page layout: Peter Kay
*Jacket illustration and uncredited
photographs:* John Allen
Road test: Courtesy of *Motor*
Printed in England, by:
J.H. Haynes & Co. Ltd

FOREWORD

The mass-produced motor car, a reality which we all take for granted today, was not even a dream in the minds of many motor manufacturers in October 1908 when Henry Ford introduced his Model T. It seems very unlikely that anyone other than Ford himself realised the true significance of this rather delicate looking, but in fact, very sturdy, automobile. An automobile which, over the following two decades, would do more than any other mechanical device before or since to change the social habits, and indeed alter the very outlook on life of the citizens of America and many other countries.

Affordable right from the start, the Model T would become ever more so as the years rolled by, thanks solely to Henry Ford's constant pursuit of his pledge to "build a car for the great multitude". With components constructed from the finest materials, produced on the most advanced tooling which could be devised, and assembled by the highest paid workers in the auto industry, the Model T was nevertheless sold at prices which no other manufacturer could match, yet generated enormous profits beyond the comprehension of many a wealthy businessman.

These profits benefited far more than the Ford family and the company stockholders, as Henry spent vast sums of his fortune on other ventures – often non-profit making. The Henry Ford Hospital, and numerous trade schools were prominent amongst these, in addition to the Henry Ford Museum and Greenfield Village where every variety of Americana has been preserved for the interest and education of future generations. Therefore, in one way or another the Model T brought freedom, prosperity, and well-being to many millions of people whose lives would have been the poorer but for its development.

For me it has been a great pleasure to delve so far back into Ford history in order to write this book, and to have had the opportunity of meeting some very nice people who today hold a Model T Ford close to their hearts. I am indebted to the members of the Model T Register of Great Britain for their interest and very great help in providing some beautiful Model Ts for photographic purposes, and my thanks therefore go to: Bob Croft, Les Croft, Tony Chesters, David Miller, John Mcloy, the Register Secretary Alan Meakin, and Simon Meakin. I am grateful also to fellow author and former Ford employee Les Geary for the loan of much historical material and Ford archive photographs from his collection, and to Howard Footitt, John Slocombe, and Keith Trotter for the loan of additional material. My thanks, too, to the magazine *Motor* for permission to reproduce the Model T road test feature. Finally, thanks to photographer John Allen who seemed to thoroughly enjoy the Model T excursions which were in such contrast to his more usual Ford GT40 work.

Michael Allen

HISTORY

Family tree

One of the more curious sights around Detroit in the late 1890s was that of Henry Ford journeying to-and-fro in his gasoline buggy. Such was the interest aroused in passers-by that Ford was obliged to tether his creation like a horse whenever he left it unattended, otherwise there was always someone whose curiosity would get the better of them and they would attempt to take a ride. There was some opposition, too, as horse owners complained that the machine frightened their animals, but the Mayor of Detroit was far-sighted enough to give Ford a special permit to use his buggy, thus making him the first licensed driver in America.

Referred to by Ford as his 'Quadricycle' (it had four bicycle-type wheels), the twin-cylinder machine represented a remarkable achievement on behalf of Ford who spent much of his spare time after work experimenting with mechanical devices which were often built from little more than scrap metal. That it worked well can be judged by the fact that after using it for a thousand miles or so Ford was able to sell it for $200 when he needed money to continue his experiments. Thankfully, it survived, and some years later Henry was able to buy it back.

By 1899, the 36 year old Henry Ford was confident enough in his ability as a mechanic to leave his job as chief engineer at the Edison Illuminating Company, in order to found the Detroit Automobile Company with financial backing from sponsors who were willing to speculate on the future of the 'horseless carriage'. This venture ended in failure. Ford himself was much to blame as he failed to come up with any worthwhile designs quickly enough, seemingly being more interested in building a publicity-seeking racing car than getting down to producing a saleable model right away. Nevertheless, one of his principal backers, timber merchant William Murphy, now sponsored a Ford-built racing car in which Henry defeated Alexander Winton's 'Bullett' over 10 miles at the Grosse Point track. This resulted in Murphy and other investors, backing Ford once again in a motor manufacturing business, with the new Henry Ford Company being formed in 1901.

Despite his ultimate goal of mass-producing an inexpensive 'peoples car', Ford was still somewhat preoccupied with ideas of racing cars at this time, and it was not long before Murphy offered him financial inducement to leave. Renamed Cadillac, the company prospered under the guidance of gifted engineer Henry M. Leland.

Meanwhile, two more Ford racers, 'Arrow' and '999' were produced, and the success of the latter in the hands of ex-racing cyclist Barney Oldfield was sufficient to tempt Detroit coal merchant Alexander Malcolmson into a trial partnership with Ford in August 1902. Malcolmson was to put up $500 whilst Ford would scheme out a production model with which it was hoped to attract sufficient investors to set up yet another manufacturing company. This time, Ford got down to business, and in June 1903 the Ford Motor Company which exists to this day was founded to produce Ford-designed automobiles in an old wagon works situated on Detroit's Mack Avenue. Ford and Malcolmson were each given a 25^1/$_2$ per cent share in the company for their part in setting up the operation, with the remaining 49 per cent divided amongst ten other men whose numbers included the Dodge brothers who were to supply engines and running gear components from their established engineering firm.

A twin-cylinder engined 'Fordmobile', designated Model A, was advertised in July 1903 at $850 for the four seat model. The first one was purchased by a doctor later that month after which orders began pouring in. At Malcolmson's suggestion, a four-cylinder Model B was added early in 1904, but at $2000 this was then a relatively highly priced car. Far more attractive, at around $1000 each according to the level of trim specified, were new Models C and F. These were, in effect, considerably refined versions of the original Model A, with similar horizontally-opposed twin-cylinder engines. So successful, in fact, were these cars that by early 1905 the Ford Motor Company was occupying new purpose-built three storey premises on the corner of Beaubin and Piquette Avenue – paid for entirely out of profits!

Nevertheless, despite the considerable success of the inexpensive models, Malcolmson, still apparently believing that real commercial success lay in low-volume production highly priced cars, insisted on an expensive six-cylinder model being added to the range. The result of this was the appearance of the large Model K which, at $2800, sold poorly, and in any case was beset with mechanical problems, as little was understood at that time about the torsional vibration problems which can occur should the crankshaft be inadequately mounted in a long six-cylinder engine. The Model K was quickly dropped, and Malcolmson (who had already invested some of his Ford dividends in a new company, Aerocar, to manufacture a car with an air cooled engine) finally sold his Ford shares to Henry in July 1906 for $175,000, thus giving Ford control over the company which bore his name.

The 1906 Model N Runabout was the best value yet at just $600. A two-seater, built on a light but sturdy chassis, the Model N featured a new 15hp four-cylinder engine capable of propelling it at speeds approaching 50mph. The Models R and S were rather more expensive De Luxe versions of the Model N, with provision for additional seating over the rear deck. With the most expensive version selling for only $750, the N/R/S range quickly established the company as the leading American car producer by selling something in the region of 15,000 examples over the period 1906–1908. Meanwhile, Henry Ford was hard at work scheming out his 'Universal Car' – the Model T Ford which, as a result of that 'T' designation, would become affectionately known worldwide as Henry's 'Tin Lizzie'.

Concept and design

There is little doubt that from the time he was old enough to have any serious ambitions, Ford's principal aim was to provide some sort of reliable mechanical transport for the great mass of ordinary people. Despite some appearances to the contrary, such as his racing cars, almost every step Ford took was towards that ultimate goal, and once having

gained full control over the most successful of the early motor manufacturing concerns there was nobody to prevent him realising that cherished dream.

Great strength was a pre-requisite for his Universal Car, for it must be able to last out its first owner's lifetime if he should indeed so wish. Any improvements incorporated into the technical specification as a result of new discoveries during production would have to be, wherever possible, interchangeable with the appropriate parts on earlier examples, so allowing an owner to update his car. All wearing parts would have to be accessible enough to facilitate easy replacement by unskilled labour with inexpensive and readily available factory produced parts which fitted perfectly – planned obsolescence and shoddy after-sales service were anathema to Henry Ford.

By one of those happy chances which occasionally occur, early in 1905 Henry Ford had been introduced to the material he needed to form the basis of his projected car. At a motor race which he was attending a French car was wrecked, and was quickly examined in detail by the inquisitive Henry Ford. The apparent great strength, yet remarkable lightness, of some components impressed him to such an extent that he kept a small piece of wreckage for analysis. Learning that the steel contained vanadium, and that its production required furnace temperatures greater than those used in the American steelmaking industry, Ford sought the advice and assistance of an English metallurgist who was conversant with the European manufacture of this steel. After being guaranteed against financial loss should they fail, a small steel company in Canton, Ohio, came up with the results Ford was seeking, so putting vanadium steel at his disposal. Experimenting further

resulted in several different grades of the new steel being made available, some of which were quickly incorporated into current production Fords where improvement in strength or lightness was desirable.

With this steelmaking knowledge, Ford, and his small design team which included C. Harold Wills and Ed 'Spider' Huff who had both been with him in the early days, and newcomer Joseph Galamb, now got down to the business of accurately working out for the first time the various ideal strength/weight requirements of the great number of individual components which make up a finished automobile. This careful analysis was to result in some twenty differing grades of steel – of which ten contained vanadium to a greater or lesser degree – going into the construction of the new Ford car at a time when automobiles generally contained about four grades of steel only.

With a tensile strength of up to $2^{1}/_{2}$ times that of anything used previously by Ford, vanadium made possible the design of a lightweight, delicate-looking chassis frame which was almost certainly the strongest 'backbone' to have gone into the construction of a motor car up to that time. At its extremities, the front crossmember accommodated the radiator attachment points, from which it was angled downwards to a flat centre section at which point was clamped the single transverse semi-elliptic leaf spring; this arrangement being pioneered previously on the Model N. The spring was attached at either end to an I-beam-section axle drop-forged from a single ingot of vanadium steel. At the rear, unlike on earlier Fords which had featured a longitudinally mounted leaf spring on either side, was another transverse leaf spring. This differed from that at the front, being of a double curvature due to the rear chassis crossmember being raised at its centre to clear the final-drive housing. These two springs were the sum total of the suspension system – there were no shock absorbers!

Of wooden construction were 24 inch diameter (front) and 23 inch diameter artillery type wheels, these being shod with 30 inch (outside diameter) x 3 inch (depth) and 30 x 3$^1/_2$ inch tyres on the front and rear respectively, giving the ground clearance necessary at a time when most 'roads' outside the townships were in reality simply the twin-rutted cart tracks beaten into the landscape by the horsedrawn vehicles of pioneering Americans. Taking into account such conditions were to result in the provision of alternative track measurements, 56 inches being the standard but with a 60 inch wide option for purchasers in southern states – 'Dixieland' farmers apparently having used somewhat wider horsedrawn vehicles than did the 'Yankees'! Simple steering arrangements featured a neat epicyclic reduction gear mounted at the top of the steering column immediately below the steering wheel, thus protecting the mechanism from the ingress of dust and dirt. The steering column was mounted on the left-hand side for the first time on an American car. The front wheels were unbraked, whilst those at the rear featured small lever operated drum brakes intended for emergency use only; a pedal-operated transmission brake was provided as the prime means of stopping under normal circumstances.

An entirely new four-cylinder sidevalve engine was conceived; its cylinder block being the finest example of casting technique seen anywhere in the American auto industry up to that time. Previously, cylinders had been cast only in pairs, integrally with the cylinder heads, with two separate twin-cylinder castings bolted onto a separate crankcase, usually of aluminium construction, in order to provide a four-cylinder unit. The new cast iron Ford block was not only in just one piece but included the upper half of the crankcase in its construction, this latter feature imparting unusual rigidity to the three crankshaft main bearing supports. The crankshaft, camshaft, and connecting rods were forged from vanadium steel, whilst the bearings in which they ran were babbit metal. The cast iron pistons featured two rings above and one below the pin; their 4 inch stroke combining with the 3$^3/_4$ inch cylinder bores to give a total swept volume of 2.9 litres.

Water jacketing extended 2$^1/_2$ inches downward around each pair of siamezed bores, whilst extending around the block at the rear only on early engines in which cooling was assisted by a gear-driven water pump, on the extended centre spindle of which was a cooling fan. The brass radiator was of multiple vertical tube construction. Experience with early production examples was to result in considerably revised cooling arrangements being introduced soon after production commenced. A revised cylinder block casting introduced water jacketing around the front of the engine whilst eliminating the water pump and so relying on the simple thermo-syphon principle for coolant circulation. The fan was now belt driven from a new crankshaft extended ahead of the front main bearing to accommodate a fan-belt pulley.

A detachable cylinder head was another notably advanced feature of the Model T engine, and this was to prove highly successful thanks to what appears to have been Ford's invention of the copper asbestos 'sandwich' type cylinder head gasket. The compression ratio was 4.5:1. Devoid of a pump, the fuel system consisted of a low-mounted Holley, or Kingston, carburettor being gravity fed from a cylindrical fuel tank mounted transversely on top of the chassis frame under the front seat position. No accelerator pedal was fitted, fuel delivery to the cylinders being controlled by a hand throttle on the steering column with a hand operated advance/retard (spark lever) on the opposite side; both being readily accessible beneath the steering wheel rim. The built-in magneto ignition system consisted of 16 magnets clamped to the flywheel which rotated past a ring of 16 coils located inside the flywheel housing. A camshaft-driven timer passed the current to four trembler coils in turn and so to the appropriate sparking plug.

A pressed steel oilpan formed the lower half of the crankcase and extended rearwards to accommodate the flywheel and Ford two-speed epicyclic transmission which shared the engine oil. Lubrication was by splash, with the flywheel being responsible for flinging the oil about. Troughs in the pan immediately below the connecting rod big ends collected sufficient oil to ensure each bearing received lubrication once every revolution.

The transmission was at first controlled by two foot pedals; one with a position for either the low forward speed (pedal fully depressed), or the high speed when the pedal was fully released, with neutral in between. The other pedal operated the transmission brake, whilst a hand lever was provided for reverse gear engagement. This system was not considered ideal, and within a short time of entering production the reverse gear lever was deleted in favour of an additional pedal placed between the other two, whilst the rear-wheel handbrake lever was incorporated into the transmission also by being modified to release the forward speed clutch as the lever was pulled backwards, so putting the car into neutral before engaging the rear brakes. Whilst this system may sound complicated at first to today's motorists, in reality it was not so. The Ford epicyclic transmission with its multiple disc steel plate clutch running in oil – rather primitive then, but not entirely dissimilar to today's automatics – eliminated the skilled business of gearchanging which called for perfect co-ordination of both right and left feet whilst double de-clutching, and simultaneously shifting the gears by hand, in those days before the conventional sliding gears had the benefit of synchromesh. Some co-ordination of throttle hand and foot pedal operation was desirable for the best results, but familiarity was quickly gained without the need for a series of formal driving lessons in order to learn how to handle a Model T. A three-pedal conversion kit was offered to the buyers of the first 800 or so two-pedal equipped cars, and almost all are thought to have been converted.

The propeller shaft was fully enclosed in a dust-proof steel case – the Ford 'torque tube' drive which would be familiar on several future generations of cars. A lightweight steel casing also housed the axle shafts and bevel final drive assembly in which the ring gear (crownwheel) was riveted to the differential housing on the earliest cars before a bolt-on arrangement was adopted early in the production run. A ratio of 3.64:1 gave overall gearing of 24.5mph/1000rpm which was well matched to the engine's torque and power outputs of approximately 80lbs/ft @ 850 rpm and 22 bhp @ 1600 rpm. Under favourable conditions the engine would attain around 1800/1900 rpm in top gear.

Upon just the one basic chassis, running gear, and drive train combination, a variety of bodywork types was to be available which would eventually give the prospective purchaser a choice of Runabout, Roadster, Tourer, Coupe, Town Car, and Sedan. The earliest examples of Model T bodywork were entirely of wooden construction, although aluminium panelled examples were produced in limited numbers alongside these before steel panelling over the wooden framework took over completely.

Mass production

Announced in October 1908 as the Ford Touring Car, at $850, the Model T Ford entered production alongside the existing, less expensive, R & S models. By the spring of 1909 the mechanical changes and improvements described previously had been incorporated in production, and the Model T would now remain fundamentally unchanged for the following 18 years. A two-seater Runabout, at $825, and a $1000 Town Car now widened the Model T range, and sales quickly overtook the R & S models which were deleted later in 1909 so as to concentrate the company's entire resources and manufacturing capacity on the production of the Model T.

A slight price rise for 1910 seemed contrary to Henry's aims but was, in fact, introduced to generate additional short-term profits which were to be ploughed back into completely new manufacturing facilities. By 1911, the 2.65 acres at Piquette Avenue had given way to 32 acres of factory space on the outskirts of Detroit at Highland Park, with plenty of room for further

expansion as the new facilities were erected on a 56 acre plot. Personnel had more than doubled from an average 1900 workers in 1908 (in which year 6000 Fords of all types had been produced), to some 4100 employees in 1911 who produced a staggering 34,000 Model Ts, a figure which, however, would seen chickenfeed only a few years hence. Prices for 1911 had been lowered to below the level of 1908-9, with further reductions for 1912 resulting in considerably more orders and an increased labour force to meet the ever rising demand.

The most significant improvement in production techniques came in 1913 with the introduction of the moving assembly lines. At first it was just the flywheel magneto which benefited, as Ford believed in trying out anything new on only a small scale before any widespread adoption. A cut in the assembly time from 20 minutes to 13 minutes was achieved for this component, with a further reduction to just 5 minutes by the simple expedient of raising the assembly line to a more comfortable height for the workers. Similar techniques applied to engine assembly now resulted in three times the previous output per man hours being achieved, and so experiments began with the final assembly of the whole car.

A chassis, accompanied by six workers, was drawn by rope and windlass across 250 ft of Highland Park floorspace, along which were situated in convenient order the remaining components and sub-assemblies necessary to produce a finished car. Whereas bringing the individual parts to the chassis for final assembly was averaging some 12$\frac{1}{2}$ man hours per car, this crudely simple experiment reduced that time to 5 hours 50 minutes, and with the mechanized system installed and everything fully integrated the final vehicle assembly time was eventually reduced to just 1 1/2 man hours.

Achieving this sort of efficiency involved removing virtually all skill from assembly operations, each being made as easy as reasonably possible, with the final assembly lines, for instance, being set at two different heights to suit squads of workers of different stature.

All assembled components were moved from station to station by mechanized means, without the assembly worker having to leave his place as, according to Ford: "Save ten steps a day for each of twelve thousand employees and you will have saved fifty miles of wasted motion and misspent energy ... pedestrianism is not a highly paid line ...". Underlining this point, an example of the often enormous savings made possible by eliminating unnecessary movement is revealed by looking at the piston and connecting rod assembly. Scrutiny of this operation, in which a team of 28 men were completing up to 175 assemblies per day, showed that the few steps each took to pick up the components, and the steps necessary to pass the finished work along resulted in each man spending some four hours a day walking even though he never left the job. A new method of working was devised so that whereas each man had been responsible for the six operations necessary to produce the finished piston/rod assembly, each man now carried out just two operations as the parts came past him on a sliding bench top. A six man team could now turn out more than 2500 assemblies per day!

Also in the quest for lower prices, some economies were made in the car itself. Certain brass fittings were superseded by steel items, the leather upholstery and trim were replaced in stages by leatherette, whilst the early bodywork colour options all gave way to just black-painted Model Ts. With prices set for 1914 at just

$550 for the full 4/5 seater Touring Car, rising to $750 for the newly introduced Coupe, Ford then rocked American industrialists by announcing that a $5 wage per 8 hour day for his workers was replacing the $2.34 wage for 9 hours' work which he had been paying in line with the other auto makers. Thought (gleefully) by Ford's competitors to be suicidal, this latest move proved to be anything but. Production soared to almost the quarter-million mark for the year, generating profits so great that at the end of the following (Ford) fiscal year a flat $50 refund was sent to everyone who had purchased a Model T that year!

With prices continuing to fall, production rose steadily over the next three years with a three-quarter million output being achieved in 1917, by which time the Touring Car was down to a mere $360. However, United States involvement in World War 1 now resulted in a decline in passenger car production as the Ford Motor Company turned over some of its resources to the manufacture of more war-like equipment. Wartime material shortages had increased costs generally, giving Ford no alternative but to raise his prices for 1918 to the levels of four years previously. Continued high material costs for some time after the war gave no chance at all of immediate price reductions at a time when the company was also spending vast sums on a completely new manufacturing

complex covering 2000 acres along the banks of Detroit's River Rouge. Although still some years away from taking over from Highland Park as the centre of Ford manufacturing, operations began at the Rouge in the summer of 1920 with the lighting up of blast furnace A. Incensed at the greed of suppliers who were maintaining wartime prices, and therefore forcing him to keep his prices artificially high, Ford was also spending millions of dollars now on the acquisition of ore mines, coalmines, timberland etc., in order to give him the fullest possible control over the supply and cost of the raw materials necessary to feed his plants.

By 1922 he had slashed his prices again, and that year at last saw the production rate pass the million mark whilst on its way to an incredible two million-plus in 1924. However, this enormous rate would not be maintained throughout the following year, as the Model T boom was coming to an end. Although considerably updated cosmetically in recent years, under the skin, apart from the (very welcome) addition of an electric starter, the Model T remained essentially as it had been in 1909; in other words, it was now simply an outdated car. Its market share began to fall from the two-thirds domination, dropping down to just one third in the latter part of 1926, and this in spite of some rejuvenation in the form of nickel-plated trim, alternative colour schemes to black, and a slightly lower line.

'Easy terms' (hire purchase facilities) were becoming widely available, so rendering rock-bottom prices somewhat less attractive than previously and were tempting buyers to purchase more expensive cars with such advanced features then as four-wheel brakes, shock absorbers etc., and 60 mph or more performance. The simple Ford could no longer compete. In May 1927, Henry Ford finally acknowledged that his beloved Model T had completed the task for which it had been created; the 64-year-old motor magnate ordered production to cease, following which he put the entire resources at his command to the job of designing and tooling up for the mass production of a thoroughly modern Ford.

The Model T in Britain

In the earliest days of the Ford Motor Company, their sales in Britain were handled by the independent Central Motor Company from their premises in Long Acre, London. Two Model As imported late in 1903 were followed by a dozen or so more during 1904 before the company came into the hands of the dynamic Percival Perry (later Lord Perry), under whose guidance it would soon be importing Fords in their hundreds. The Model B proved popular as a basis for London taxis, whilst the Model N in 1906 established the company as a major car importer into Britain.

Within only a matter of days following its October 1908 introduction in the United States, the Model T was on display at Olympia's London Motor Show where some 250 orders were taken on the Ford stand. Sales continued increasing to such a great extent that Perry was prompted to suggest to Henry Ford in 1910 that the time had come for the formation of an English subsidiary of what was by now the most successful American auto-making concern. Upon the suggestion being accepted, Perry found himself at the head of the new Ford Motor Company (England) Ltd., with premises on London's Shaftesbury Avenue through which Model Ts would be imported until such time as the new company had established a suitable manufacturing base.

A disused carriage works on Manchester's western outskirts at Trafford Park attracted Perry's attention, the suitable looking premises having the added attraction of being situated close to Salford Docks which formed the terminus of the Manchester Ship Canal. Late in 1911, Model Ts shipped direct from America in CKD (unassembled) form were being docked here, and in October that year the first of the British-assembled Fords was leaving the Trafford Park works.

3000 sales were made in 1912, and more than double that number the following year. By 1914 Trafford Park was already Europe's largest car producer, building cars at twice the rate of any other British manufacturer with the moving assembly lines now being introduced in Britain following their advent at Highland Park, Michigan, adding considerably to Manchester's productive capacity.

Local resources were being included now in British manufacture, particularly in respect of bodywork and trim items, which resulted in some of these Fords becoming more British-built rather than just British-assembled cars; this was certainly to become the case in respect of many of the Model Ts which would see service in the First World War. Although used by the military as a scout car, machine gun carrier, and even as a supply car which could double as a mobile workshop, the Model T's major role in the conflict quickly became that of an ambulance. With its rugged qualities and excellent ground clearance the Model T was ideal for transporting the wounded from the front lines, and in the early days the standard Touring Car was widely used for these duties before ambulance conversions for the Ford chassis appeared. Trafford Park introduced its own purpose-built ambulance in 1915, featuring wood and canvas rear bodywork designed to accommodate two stretcher cases

or alternatively, four sitting patients. A driver plus attendant/nurse usually formed the ambulance crew. Production of this Model T variant eventually reached more than 100 vehicles per day.

With hostilities over, Trafford Park was soon wholly in the business of meeting civilian needs once again, and at a rate of production which enabled the Model T to satisfy no less than 41% of the expanding British market. A Model T Delivery Car (light van) was a production variant, and converting Model Ts for a variety of roles was quite common practice with pick-up type rear bodywork in place of the dickey seat being popular and extremely useful on the inexpensive Runabout model. The relatively short wheelbase however was a severely limiting factor in these conversions, but the ingenious Baico '1 Tonner' chassis conversion overcame the problem by virtue of an extended chassis and additional rear axle. The original axle remained in position, but clamped rigidly to the chassis and minus its rear wheels which were replaced with sprockets. These formed part of a chain drive mechanism to the new rear axle suspended on longitudinally mounted leaf springs attached further aft on the extended chassis rails. Several quite commodious mobile homes were built on Baico-modified chassis with all-up weights of up to two tons being recorded, at which the Model T would struggle manfully to maintain 20 mph or so while on the move.

The availability in Britain from mid 1919 of Ford's own long wheelbase Model TT 1 ton truck chassis, which had gone on sale in America the previous year, gave the company its first real foothold in the growing commercial vehicle market. In addition to the Ford vans and trucks available from the factory, on this chassis were a variety of alternatives from outside bodybuilders.

Coach tours were becoming a popular pastime in postwar Britain, and the long-wheelbase Ford lent itself well to the role of motor coach. Many operators in the 1920s combined these activities with that of haulage during the weekdays, and completely detachable bus and truck bodies which could quickly replace one another were by no means uncommon. Giving the best of both worlds, and designed specifically for the Ford chassis was the Gray-Podmore dual purpose body which came on the market in 1921. The steel-panelled full width open bodywork featured three rows of twin seats down each side leaving a narrow central gangway. Passenger access was via a wide nearside front door, and two additional passengers could be accommodated alongside the driver on the front bench seat to give a 14 passenger capacity in the vehicle's weekend role. A folding hood was standard equipment to give protection from the elements when necessary. Removing the seats aft of the front bench gave a wide, high-sided open lorry, with access for loading at the rear via a detachable tailgate. The folded hood was cleverly arranged so that it could be swung down to below the floor line at the rear during loading operations; it could, of course, be used in the raised position as on the coach should the lorry load warrant the additional protection.

Coachwork versatility such as this resulted in the Gray-Podmore Model TT finding widespread employment outside its two principal roles of motor coach or lorry. With just some of the seats removed the vehicle was an ideal shooting brake, and also proved eminently suitable for outside caterers to transport waiters along with the food, cutlery, crockery etc. to social functions. Hoteliers, and even undertakers, were amongst many others who appreciated this model's adaptability.

Overall, however, the Model T's market share began to drop at this time, due in no small measure to the curious horsepower tax method of financing Britain's road building programme. With a car's horsepower being calculated (for taxation purposes) on the engine's bore size only, the taxation imposed was heavily biased against the large-bore Ford, but being levied at just a few shillings per horsepower had had little effect on the Model T in its earlier days. A savage increase to £1 per horsepower in 1921, however, resulted in the Model T owner now being charged a hefty £23 per year for the privilege of taking his Ford on the road, and this sharp increase in running costs considerably offset the Ford's unbeatable first cost advantage which it held over everything else in Britain at that time.

Nevertheless, the 250,000th British Model T was produced during 1925, with a further 50,000 being added to that total by the late summer of 1927 when the last Model T to be completed left Trafford Park.

Accessories

The Model T Ford has been variously described as 'stark', a 'bare-bones automobile' etc. etc., and indeed it was these things in many respects as a result of its creator's desire to offer a car constructed from the finest materials available, yet selling at the lowest price possible. Therefore, luxury trimmings, non-essential gadgets, and sophisticated components where a simpler part would suffice had no place in Henry's thinking as he schemed out his car for the multitudes.

However, with tens of thousands of Model Ts quickly multiplying into millions, it was no surprise that many owners were interested in improving the specification, or perhaps the equipment level of the rugged Ford which had become a valued member of the family and looked like remaining so for many years. So it was that the 'bare-bones' Ford gave birth to another whole new industry – that of the independent auto-accessory manufacturers.

Over its 19-year production run some 5000 accessory items would become available for the Model T, with every aspect of the car coming in for some sort of attention or another. Coil and distributor ignition systems, and 'non fouling' spark plugs were remedies offered for the Model T with misfiring problems, and a whole variety of replacement carburettors, which would improve its gasoline-mileage, or pep-up a lethargic Model T, became available. Thus revived, perhaps the Ford would pull a higher gear and, if so, there were replacement crownwheel and pinion sets which would allow a healthy Model T to run at 55 mph.

Long before Ford offered the electric self-starter there were mechanical devices with which to turn the engine over from the comfort of the driving seat. For those who didn't really mind cranking the car from the front a 'non-kick device' from the Non-Kick Device Co. (who else?) of Kansas City was, according to their advertisement: "Better than insurance because it prevents sprained wrists, broken arms, with their pain and suffering, inconvenience and doctor bills." – all this anguish was being saved for just $2.50! Even so, these aids wouldn't help the fuel mixture on those bitter winter mornings, and on such occasions it would seem that one of the numerous, and often quite ingenious, inlet manifold heaters could be of real help in coaxing a Model T engine into life. Other useful winter accessories were radiator covers in either leather or canvas, and a variety of interior heating apparatus, the most rudimentary consisting of just a simple metal shield placed over the exhaust manifold in order to deflect the heat backwards in the hope that it would filter through into the body.

Aiding passenger comfort in a different respect, by giving some assistance to the Model T's road springs, were shock absorbers which came in many shapes and sizes. The more sophisticated of these incorporated auxiliary springs in their design, whilst the simplest, advertised as 'Rebound Checks' were nothing more than a stout leather strap with buckle fastening for fitting around the road spring and axle. A 'Little Steersman' attachment to the front end arrangements consisted of a helical spring affixed transversely to the axle and steering gear; a useful aid to self-centering, this was also effective in eliminating wander by keeping the front wheels in perfect alignment when the Model T was suffering from well-worn steering joints.

Clamp-on bumper bars, electric sidelamps, exhaust deflectors, rubber foot-pedal pads, floor mats, instruments, seat covers etc., etc., all enabled the owner who had fallen in love with his Tin Lizzie to dress her up in the manner of an expensive automobile. And how well she deserved it, too.

The Model T in motor sport

With the Model T just nicely into quantity production, wealthy mine owner Robert Guggenheim could not have picked a better time from Ford's point of view to promote a New York – Seattle endurance race in June 1909 as part of the Yukon – Alaskan Exposition. Here was the perfect opportunity for Henry to demonstrate his new car's rugged qualities.

With many infant auto-manufacturing concerns in the United States a large entry was expected, but this was at the time of the famous Selden Patent controversy in which Henry was leading the fight against having to pay royalties in respect of an opportunist patent taken out years earlier by a patent attorney for a 'self propelled road locomotive', for which, however, no workable design had been schemed out by Selden. The 83 companies who were meekly paying up refused to enter the endurance race alongside Ford who they considered to be an 'unlicensed' manufacturer; this excuse hopefully covering up the fact that they didn't exactly fancy the idea of the inexpensive Ford beating them out of sight. The changing of any major parts during the race was prohibited, and this doubtless scared off many contestants too; but not Ford who claimed: "Ford will stay in even if they prohibit tyre replacements and spark plug renewals". And so it was that just five cars – two Fords crewed by Ford employees Kulick/Harper and Scott/Smith, a Shawmut, an Acme, and an imported Itala – made the start line in New York on June 1st, with the cheapest of the opposition costing five times as much as a Ford, whilst all boasting engines in the 40 to 50 hp category.

Ahead lay more than 4000 miles along which many checkpoints had to be visited, but with no stipulated route between the towns out west where there were still no roads as such; the crews would simply have to judge which old trail, or perhaps even direct cross-country route would hopefully serve them best. There were few incidents on the eastern leg between New York and St Louis until heavy rains in Illinois affected all competitors. Although itself behind schedule, the Shawmut took an early lead, getting into St Louis two hours ahead of the Fords which were running together in the early stages. Rain, that turned the tracks into quagmires, continued for days as the contestants made their way across the Great Plains.

The two Fords parted company in Kansas on June 8th when Kulick decided to take a good night's rest, but met up again next day when Kulick's Ford came upon that of Scott and Smith stranded in a stream after sliding down an embankment. Kulick soon towed them clear, but by now the Shawmut had a good lead, although the Itala and Acme were already well behind.

Kulick stopped over in Denver to service his Ford, and was four hours behind Scott's car and the Shawmut when those two left Cheyenne neck and neck. A great effort by Kulick now saw him up with the leaders by the time they reached the River Platte. The road bridge was washed out, and so the two Fords and the Shawmut made a perilous crossing by the Union Pacific Railroad trestle bridge (the race rules had foreseen this possibility and therefore banned both the riding on railroad cars and the carrying or fitting of a set of flanged wheels). Scott's Ford and the Shawmut apparently bumped their way across the railroad ties (sleepers) unscathed, but Kulick's Ford suffered a broken wheel getting across, so losing more time before getting it repaired.

Scott's Ford went into a ditch somewhere in Wyoming, damaging an axle, and by the time the two Fords were back in action the tough Shawmut was some hours ahead, and causing the Ford crews considerable concern. Nevertheless, after more than two weeks on the trail the three cars were together again, and the weary crews agreed to hole up in a small town for a night's rest before beginning the battle anew, level pegging, the following day. Kulick now opened up a considerable distance between himself and the others, only to lose it all and more after getting lost in Idaho. Three weeks out from New York it was the

Scott/Smith Ford in the lead on June 21st. Disaster almost overtook the leader when a gas station attendant spilled fuel over the car and suddenly the scanty bodywork burst into flames. Onlookers rallied round and helped beat out the fire, and Scott held on to his lead with just the mountainous country east of Seattle still to negotiate.

There was still much snow on the high ground in the northwestern region even in June, and Scott's Ford had to be dug out of deep snow on one occasion before finally making it into Seattle on June 23rd, 17 hours ahead of the Shawmut in second place. Kulick's Ford had suffered a badly damaged axle through striking a rock hidden in the deep snows which had held up Scott, and lost another day or so locating and fitting a replacement axle before arriving in Seattle on the 25th. The replacement part did, of course, lead to disqualification, with the third place eventually going to the Acme which came in some days later. The Itala failed to finish.

A Ford employee almost from the very beginning, Frank Kulick was amongst the spectators who witnessed Henry Ford set up a new land speed record of 91 mph with his fearsome machine 'Arrow' on the frozen Lake St. Clair in January 1904, and later that year the enthusiastic youngster was racing a Ford-built machine himself with full company backing. A high speed crash in a Model K racer in 1907, from which by all accounts he was extremely lucky to escape with his life, had nevertheless resulted in a badly broken leg which was to leave him with a permanent limp. Alarmed at the risks involved as cars were getting faster, Henry Ford had then curtailed the company's racing activities.

However, the New York – Seattle affair had whetted Henry's appetite once more, and in 1910 Kulick was regularly in action on the dirt tracks with a stripped

down Model T. In his hands the Ford was enjoying considerable success, usually, thanks to its lightweight construction, beating cars of far greater horsepower. But this was not to last very long. As the sport became more organized, classifications were introduced based on purchase price, or on engine displacement but with a minimum weight (much higher than the Model T's) in each engine capacity class. Thus, the Model Ts were effectively relegated to simply racing amongst themselves, as the only others in the same low-price category were pathetic twin-cylinder jobs not even quick enough to eat the Ford's dust. An attempt to enter the 1913 Indianapolis 500 was barred because the Model T-based car was too light; and in any case, sadly, there were already plenty of fatalities taking place in auto racing. Henry was not at all happy about the possibility of the Ford Motor Company becoming associated with that unfortunate aspect of the sport, and so the decision was taken to withdraw completely from competition.

Although works-entered Model Ts would not race again, within a few years hotted-up Fords, literally in their thousands, would become the poor man's racing car on the countless unlicensed dirt tracks of America. Suspension lowering kits, and sleek racing bodywork from many sources became available with which the budding racing driver could transform a cheap secondhand Model T out of all

recognition. Providing the power to match these Speedster's looks were numerous cylinder head conversions and appropriately modified carburettor installations ranging from mildly reworked standard items to a sophisticated double overhead camshaft 16-valve job. The latter was the ulltimate in a whole series of cylinder heads designed for the Model T Ford by Arthur and Louis Chevrolet, and known as the Frontenac heads. These came also with either pushrod operated overhead valves or a single overhead camshaft 8-valve set up.

There were many others, too, such as the Rajo, or the Roof-Laurel, but the Fronty-Fords were by far the most popular, with some 10,000 of these cylinder heads being sold during the 1920s, although not all were, it seems, actually destined to race, as the Fronty-Fords were apparently popular with the bootleggers of that era as a reliable means of outrunning the revenue agents!

Success review

For more than 40 years after production ceased the Model T Ford remained the biggest-selling automobile in history, and was generally accepted as being the world's most successful car. It had firmly established the Ford Motor Company as the most successful independent manufacturer in the history of motoring, whilst making Henry Ford one of the wealthiest and, perhaps, the most famous industrialist of his time. Even today, 60 years after the last Model T left the assembly lines it is second in total sales only to the Volkswagen Beetle of much later years, and that car, whose conception was actually inspired by the Model T's success, took many years longer to reach the Ford's production figure while undergoing far more technical changes in the process. But, the Model T was very much more than just a big-selling car; it was the tangible result of its creator's unswerving pursuit of his idea that any man holding down a steady job should, if he so wished, be able to have his own new car. The Model T succeeded in turning that idea into reality far more than just the 15,000,000 times represented by its total sales, for its success forced many other manufacturers to adopt streamlined production methods enabling them to add inexpensive models to their product range.

Without Henry Ford and his Model T, the ''great multitude'' of which he spoke would without doubt have waited decades longer before being able to enjoy that wonderful freedom of personal transportation.

EVOLUTION

Evolution

Introduced on October 1st, 1908, the original Model T Touring Cars, at $850, are nevertheless usually considered to be 1909 cars, as Ford's model year, like that of so many other manufacturers since, generally started some months before the new calender year began. Whilst the model year could more or less be relied upon in respect of styling and, after the first year, bodywork options, technical changes were usually incorporated soon after being devised. This often resulted in some overlapping until the remaining stocks of earlier components were exhausted if the change in specification was for manufacturing or supply reasons, rather than in respect of reliability.

By mid 1909, the Touring Car had been joined by the Roadster ($825), the hard-top Coupe ($950) and the $1000 Town Car with Landaulet rear bodywork. The small range of colour options available consisted of Carmine red, grey, black, and Brewster green. The originally optional windscreen and hood for the open cars (Touring and Roadster) was included in the standard specifications for 1910, as was the

acetylene headlamp set which, curiously, remained an option on the closed Coupe and Town Car. A Torpedo Runabout, with raked-back windscreen and lowered steering column giving a rather speedier look to this variation of the Model T theme, was new this year, but destined for only a short production run.

Changes during 1911 were the standardization of steel-panelled bodywork, the introduction of a new crankcase/transmission oilpan with an access panel beneath the connecting rods, and a new transmission top cover giving easier access for transmission band adjustment. The Ford Delivery Car made its appearance for 1912, whilst the regular Roadster model was also offered as a Commercial Roadster with a flat rear deck on which small loads could be carried once the detachable 'mother-in-law' seat had been removed.

Announced in November 1912, the 1913 models were characterized by the raked-back treatment of the lower section of the split windscreen, and rather more smoothly finished bodywork. Economies were to be seen in the removal of much of the brasswork; the side and tail lamp bodies were now painted metal, as was the windscreen frame, although the charming brass radiator remained. Confined just to the door trims at this stage, leatherette made its appearance as an inexpensive trim material. For 1914 the Model T was to carry on virtually unchanged. However, only black-painted cars would be available because black paint dried more quickly than any other colour, and drying time was consistent and fast enough to allow body production to dovetail neatly into the new totally integrated mass-production arrangements.

For 1915 a new drophead Coupelet replaced the hardtop Coupe, and the first Ford Sedan

made its appearance. Of two door configuration, the Sedan offered closed car amenities for up to five people, and was interesting in that the doors were positioned centrally in the body sides, so equalling the convenience, or otherwise, of ease of entry and exit between the front and rear seat occupants. Appearing first on the Coupelet and Sedan, bodywork, on which a front cowl curved gracefully from the engine compartment to the windscreen, with the latter being repositioned slightly rearwards whilst readopting an upright stance, became a characteristic feature of the entire range during the early part of 1915, after which the bodywork remained almost unchanged for several years. Electric headlamps, drawing their current from an improved flywheel magneto, were another notable advance this year over previous Fords, whilst redesigned side and tail lamps, still oil lit, and louvres in the engine side covers were other changes identifying a 1915 Model T. Inside, leatherette had now taken over completely apart from small panels on the seat sides adjacent to the doors where potential wear was at its greatest.

A 'new' Model T appeared in August 1916, on which the remaining brass trim, including the 'antique' radiator, was replaced by painted metal. The new, slightly taller radiator and matching hood which faired straight into the cowl gave these latest Model Ts a cleaner, more modern appearance. Accompanying these changes was a massive price reduction right across the range, from $45 off the Runabout (down to $345) to $100 off the Sedan which was now listed at $640. The best-selling Touring Car was now just $360.

An enclosed Coupe, lower-built than the earlier Coupe, replaced the Coupelet for 1919, whilst the rather poor-selling Town Car was discontinued. Optional equipment this year, albeit on the Coupe and Sedan only, was a self starter. On the cars so fitted, this at last resulted in a dynamo and battery appearing on the Model T Ford. Changes to the flywheel were necessary to incorporate the starter ring gear, and to the cylinder block in order to mount the generator, with the modified block eventually becoming standard whether starting equipment was specified or not. This, in turn, led to the electric starter becoming optional throughout the range.

Demountable wheel rims were another option for 1919 which removed the chore of repairing and replacing an inner tube by the roadside in the event of a punctured tyre. Prices now of $500 for the Runabout, rising to $775 for the Sedan were simply due to the effects the war had upon the cost of materials.

Late in 1922 the Touring Car received a new 'one man' top which, according to the catalogues anyway, was easier to raise and lower than that of the earlier Touring Cars. A raked-back windscreen accompanied the new top, and was also to be seen now on the Runabout, giving these Model Ts a slightly more streamlined appearance. Taking over from the centre door Sedan were a new Tudor (two door) model with the doors situated at the front, and an altogether more convenient Fordor (four door) Sedan. These 1923 models continued virtually unchanged right through to 1925; unchanged, that is, apart from the prices which, as sales reached their fantastic peak, fell to an all time low for 1925 of just $260 (Runabout), $290 (Touring Car), $520 (Coupe), $580 (Tudor Sedan), and $660 for the Fordor Sedan. And at that level the previously optional demountable wheel rims, and a spare tyre and rim were also included.

For 1926 came the up-dated Model Ts with which Henry Ford hoped to prove that the model could remain in production for ever. Adjusting the crown of the transverse leaf springs and raising the front wheel spindles slightly resulted in a lower chassis, which, with $4^1/2$ in. x 21 in. balloon tyres, and slightly longer bodies (except the Fordor Sedan) gave an appreciably more modern look to the ageing Ford. Curiously, the Fordor Sedan also retained the wooden-framed construction and the under-seat fuel tank, whereas all other variants were manufactured wholly in steel and featured a scuttle-mounted fuel tank with the filler immediately beneath the cowl vent. Whilst the open cars retained the all-black finish, including the radiator shell, the closed cars were glamorized considerably with the Coupe and Tudor Sedan being finished in Channel Green, and the Fordor Sedan in Windsor Maroon. A nickel-plated radiator further enhanced the closed cars' appearance.

A wider transmission brake band, and increased diameter brake drums now housing asbestos-lined shoes rather than the plain cast iron variety as before, were dictated due to the Model T having put on weight in its latest guise. Lightweight pistons upped the engine's power output slightly in the hope that it too could cope with the heavier car, whilst a lowering of the steering ratio would ease the driver's burden at manoeuvring speeds; this change, however, made necessary more by the adoption of balloon tyres. Further colour options, now including the open cars, were new for 1927, during the early part of which wire wheels became standard equipment on the closed Coupe whilst remaining optional on the range as a whole.

Price increases had accompanied the up-dated cars, and at the finish in mid 1927 the range consisted of the Runabout ($360), Touring Car ($380), Coupe ($485), Tudor Sedan ($495), and Fordor Sedan at $545.

Approximate end of year engine numbers

Engines installed in cars when new were numbered consecutively, and this number was also regarded as the car number. Therefore, on surviving cars known to be still fitted with their original engine this number may be used to determine the approximate date of manufacture. On all but the very earliest cars, the engine number is stamped into the cylinder block on the left-hand side adjacent to the bottom hose connection.

December 1908	309
December 1909	14161
December 1910	34900
December 1911	88900
December 1912	171300
December 1913	370400
December 1914	611100
December 1915	1029200
December 1916	1614600
December 1917	2449100
December 1918	2831400
December 1919	3659970
December 1920	4698420
December 1921	5638071
December 1922	6953071
December 1923	9008381
December 1924	10999901
December 1925	12990055
December 1926	14619254
Final number	15007033

One of the earliest Model Ts to have survived, this 1909 Touring Car is displayed in the Henry Ford Museum at Dearborn. Although featuring the very early two-pedal, two-lever controls, this car is said to have been converted to this original specification retrospectively when being restored for display.

Red paintwork also shows off well the rare 1913 British-bodied Model T, on which the curved mudguards were ahead of their time in respect of Model T development.

The accessory engine temperature gauge sits atop a filler cap style referred to as the 'dogbone' by Model T enthusiasts.

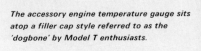

Although non-standard for its year due to the green paintwork, the restoration of this 1915 Tourer, with its polished brass details, is truly magnificent. At over 70 years old, it still provides a great way to enjoy some sunshine motoring – the author has had the privilege of riding in this car and can confirm that it runs as well as it looks.

By the time this Model T was built, black paintwork had become the only colour on offer. It has been enhanced at a later date on this example by the neatly carried out gold striping and bright red wheels. The classic front threequarter view shows Henry's masterpiece off to perfection ...

... whilst from the rear, too, the beautifully restored EL 1733 looks fine.

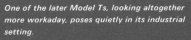
One of the later Model Ts, looking altogether more workaday, poses quietly in its industrial setting.

Unadorned black can indeed be beautiful. Spick and span, this lovely centre door Sedan looks all set to convey its passengers to some elegant social function.

Varnished woodwork in conjunction with alternative colours to black gives a most attractive appearance to these particular commercial variations of the ubiquitous Ford. Of 1925 vintage, XD 8457 is still quite a youngster by Model T standards.

*Well, isn't that just dandy – a Model T speedster.
Just the thing for the American youth at the
height of the Roaring Twenties.*

Still very much the same under the skin as the original 1909 model displayed in the Henry Ford Museum, and even wearing a similar red colour scheme enhanced by polished brasswork, this 1923 Touring Car has an altogether more modern appearance than the earlier Touring Cars.

By this time, drivers of the Touring Car had the benefit of their own door, although the unchanged position of the handbrake lever did not make for stylish exits!

Looking like it means business, DS 7086 is impressive when viewed from the rear.

SPECIFICATION

Specification

Manufacturer	Ford Motor Company.
Type designation	Model T.
Built	Dearborn, Michigan, USA. Final assembly also at various overseas plants.
Number built	15,007,033

Engine

Cylinder block	Cast iron. Cast integrally with upper half of crankcase. Four cylinders in line, bores siamezed in pairs with cooling-water jacketing encircling each pair of cylinders.
Cylinder head	Cast iron, detachable.
Valve gear layout	Side, operated by low-mounted camshaft gear-driven from crankshaft nose. Non-adjustable tappets.
Crankshaft	Three main bearings, non-counterbalanced.
Capacity	2890cc
Bore & stroke	95 mm x 101.5 mm
Compression ratio	4.5:1 (early), lowered progressively (due to deteriorating quality of gasoline brought about by oil companies' efforts to meet totally unforeseen demands) to 4.0:1.
Maximum power	22bhp @ 1600rpm (4.5:1 compression ratio). 20bhp @ 1600 rpm (4.0:1 compression ratio).
Maximum torque	80lbs/ft @ 850rpm.

Fuel system

	Gravity feed to single updraught carburettor.
Carburettor	Holley; Kingston; or Ford.
Fuel tank capacity	8 gallons (approx).

Ignition system

	Flywheel magneto, timer, and trembler coils.

Transmission

	Ford epicyclic (planetary) two forward speeds and reverse, pedal operated. Enclosed propeller shaft (torque tube drive) to bevel final drive/differential assembly.
Final Drive ratio	3.64:1
Overall gearing	24.5mph/1000rpm (high) 11.2mph/1000rpm (low)

Suspension	Non-independent. Single transverse leaf spring front and rear. Additional front and rear axle location by radius rods.
Steering	Epicyclic reduction gear.
Brakes	Pedal operated transmission brake. Lever operated emergency drum brakes on rear wheels only.
Wheels & tyres	Wooden spoke artillery type wheels, non detachable. De-mountable outer rims available later as optional extra. Wire wheels optional during last year of production. Straight-sided tubed tyres 30 in. x 3 in. front, 30 in. x $3^1/_2$ in. rear. $4^1/_2$ in. x 21 in. ballon tyres available later with either artillery or wire wheels.
Electrical system	None on early models other than flywheel magneto, 6 volt battery and dynamo for later models with full electric lighting and starter motor.
Bodywork	Wood framed. Wood panelled very early models, steel panelled thereafter.
Body types	Runabout; Tourer; Coupe; Coupelet; Town/Landaulet; centre door Sedan; two door Sedan (Tudor); four door Sedan (Fordor); delivery van.
Dimensions	Wheelbase 8ft 4in. Track 4 ft 8in.
Weight	13cwt (approx) Runabout. 16cwt (approx) Fordor Sedan.

Performance

Maximum speed	45mph (approx).
0–30mph	16 seconds (approx).
Fuel consumption	25 – 35mpg.

720   *December 19, 1951.*   The Motor

Christmas Road Test No. 19/51

Makers: Ford Motor Co. (England) Ltd., Trafford Park, Manchester.

(Test car submitted by Dagenham Motors, Ltd., 56, Park Lane, London, W.1)

Make: Ford.   **Type:** Model T (1912) 2-seater Runabout.

Dimensions and Seating

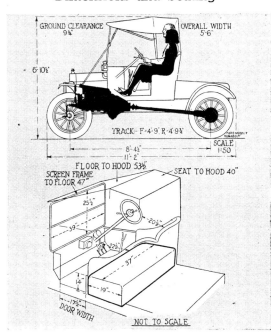

GROUND CLEARANCE 9¾"   OVERALL WIDTH 5'-6"

6'-10½"

TRACK - F-4'-9" R-4'-9¾"   FORD MODEL T RUNABOUT   SCALE 1:50

8'-4½"
11'-2"

FLOOR TO HOOD 53½"   SEAT TO HOOD 40"
SCREEN FRAME TO FLOOR 47"

25½"
-39"   20½"
22½"
37"
14"   19"
-17½"
DOOR WIDTH   NOT TO SCALE

Test Conditions

Cold, damp weather, stiff breeze, smooth tarmac surface, Pool petrol.
Windscreen fully erect during tests.

Test Data

ACCELERATION TIMES on Two Ratios

	High	Low
10-30 m.p.h.	12.8 secs.	—
20-40 m.p.h.	31.5 secs.	—

ACCELERATION TIMES Through Gears

0-20 m.p.h.	8.5 secs.
0-30 m.p.h.	15.3 secs.
0-40 m.p.h.	35.8 secs.
Standing Quarter Mile	32.9 secs.

FUEL CONSUMPTION

35.0 m.p.g. at constant 20 m.p.h.
32.0 m.p.g. at constant 30 m.p.h.
Overall consumption .. .. 28.5 m.p.g.

HILL CLIMBING (at steady speeds)

Max. high gear speed on 1 in 20	35 m.p.h.
Max. high gear speed on 1 in 15	32 m.p.h.
Max. gradient on high gear	1 in 11.1 (Tapley 200 lb./ton)

BRAKES at 30 m.p.h.

0.41g retardation (=73 ft. stopping distance) with 50 lb. pedal pressure

MAXIMUM SPEEDS

Mean maximum speed in high gear approx. 42 m.p.h.
Max. speed in low gear .. .. 16 m.p.h.

WEIGHT

Unladen kerb weight	13¾ cwt.
Front/rear weight distribution	49/51
Weight laden as tested	16¾ cwt.

INSTRUMENTS

Speedometer at 30 m.p.h.	16% fast
Distance recorder	3% slow

In Brief

Price, in 1912, £135 (inclusive of hood and windscreen).
Capacity .. .. .. 2,890 c.c.
Unladen kerb weight .. 13¾ cwt.
Fuel consumption .. 28.5 m.p.g.
Maximum speed .. .. 42 m.p.h.
Maximum speed on 1 in 20 gradient .. .. .. 35 m.p.h.
Maximum top gear gradient 1 in 11.1
Acceleration
10-30 m.p.h. in top .. 12.8 secs.
0-40 m.p.h. through gears 35.8 secs.
Gearing 24.5 m.p.h. in top at 1,000 r.p.m. 92 m.p.h. at 2,500 ft. per min. piston speed.

Specification

Engine

Cylinders	4
Bore	95 mm.
Stroke	101.5 mm.
Cubic capacity	2,890 c.c.
Piston area	44 sq. in.
Valves	Side
Max. power	approx. 20 b.h.p.
at	approx. 1,800 r.p.m.
Piston speed at max. b.h.p.	approx. 1,200 ft. per min.
Carburetter	Holley (updraught choke)
Ignition	Flywheel magneto (trembler coils for starting)
Fuel feed	By gravity from tank under seat
Oil circulation	By splash from flywheel

Transmission

Clutch	Multiple steel disc
High gear (direct)	3.64
Low gear (epicyclic)	10.0
Reverse gear (epicyclic)	14.5
Propeller shaft	Enclosed in torque tube
Final drive	Bevel

Chassis

Brakes .. Foot, enclosed band brake on transmission; hand, internal expanding brakes on rear wheels

Suspension front	Transverse leaf
rear	Transverse leaf
Shock absorbers	Nil
Tyres	B.T.R., 765×105

Steering

Steering gear	Epicyclic
Turning circle	37 ft.
Turns of steering wheel, lock to lock	1¼

Performance factors (at laden weight as tested)

Piston area, sq. in. per ton	52.5
Specific displacement, litres per ton mile	4,230

Described in "The Motor," November 9, 1911.

Maintenance

Fuel tank: 8 gallons. **Sump (engine and gearbox):** 6-8 pints, approx. S.A.E. 20 (NOT graphited, to avoid shorting flywheel magneto). **Rear axle:** Fill every 500 miles with grease (in extremely cold weather, use heavy oil). **Steering Gear:** Grease every 5,000 miles. **Radiator:** 3 gallons (drain tap). **Chassis Lubrication:** Apply oilcan to 12 oilers, and screw down 6 grease cups one turn, every 200 miles. **Front hubs:** Re-grease every 500 miles. **Ignition:** Clean and re-oil commutator every 500 miles. **Spark plug gap:** 1/32 in. **Tappet clearances (cold):** Inlet and exhaust 1/32 in. **Front wheel toe-in:** Nil. **Tyre pressures:** Front and rear, 55 lb.

Ref. U.S-B/29/12-51.

December 19, 1951.

The **Motor**

—The FORD Model T 1912 Torpedo Runabout

TOURING TRIM—With two comfortable seats, behind a large windscreen, the upper half of which may be folded down in summer, the Ford Runabout is sufficiently high-built to give an excellent view over walls and hedgerows.

A CLASSIC amongst cars, the Ford model T (of which 15 million examples were built between 1907 and 1927) contributed an immense amount to the popularizing of motoring in all parts of the world. Inexpensive and simple, yet with a great capacity for hard work, this famous car was built to daringly unorthodox designs, and although many of its features are nowadays unfamiliar it is also in some respects still modern. It was with immense interest that we recently took over a 1912 example of this model from Dagenham Motors Ltd., an example not merely immaculate but also in excellent mechanical condition, to sample it against a background of 1951 road conditions.

Many readers will be more than familiar with this type of car, but for the benefit of those (like the testers) of a generation which has grown up since the model T was taxed off the roads of Britain, some mechanical details must be recapitulated.

The engine is astonishingly modern looking, a compact 23 h.p. monobloc side-valve four cylinder, with detachable cylinder head and 3-bearing crankshaft, having external inlet and exhaust manifolds on the right-hand side; mounted in unit with the engine is the clutch and 2-speed epicyclic gearbox assembly. Behind the gearbox there is a torque tube to a rear axle incorporating the conventional bevel gearing and differential. These mechanical parts are mounted in a simple frame having channel section side members, transverse leaf springs and radius arms providing for front and rear axle location.

Our tests of the Ford were made in frosty December weather, but starting from cold proved commendably certain, albeit the procedure to be followed was more lengthy than is commonly necessary nowadays. Owing to drag in the transmission, when the oil which lubricates this and the engine is really cold, it is first necessary to jack up the easily-accessible rear axle. With the handbrake half on and the choke control wire, which extends through the radiator, pulled, the engine is given three or four pull-ups by means of the permanently-in-position starting handle, to prime the cylinders

Then, with the ignition switch turned to "battery," the hand throttle set about 4 notches open and the ignition control advanced 4 notches, a single sharp pull of the starting handle should set the engine running : the ignition may immediately be switched over from the trembler coils to "magneto," and after a few minutes warming up of the engine it should be possible to overcome transmission oil drag with the footbrake and safely to lower the rear axle from its jack. It should be emphasized that the car can be left standing for a considerable number of hours without requiring to be jacked up for safe re-starting.

Set running, and warmed up to a reasonable extent, the engine idles completely reliably and with a reasonable degree of smoothness. It is controlled by the driver through the medium of a pair of levers which move with pleasing smoothness over notched quadrants below the wooden-rimmed steering wheel, the left-hand lever regulating throttle opening and the right-hand lever ignition timing.

To drive away is simple enough, once the unconventional control system is clearly understood—experience with other types of car is apt to have produced instinctive reactions which need to be un-learned before the model T is handled with proper dexterity.

Three pedals are provided, and all of them work on the enclosed transmission unit. The right-hand pedal operates a normal transmission brake : the central one is the reversing pedal : the left-hand pedal is the low gear, neutral and high gear control. Of these, the first mentioned requires no explanation, and the second will be referred to later : the third is designed to engage high gear when it is released, to give neutral when it is half depressed, and to select low gear when it is fully depressed. The handbrake lever is

POWER UNIT AND CONTROLS—The 2.9-litre four-cylinder engine is notably modern looking, this model having pioneered the use of a removable cylinder head. The controls comprise three pedals for forward gears, reverse gear and the brake in the epicyclic transmission respectively: a handbrake which de-clutches the engine in the first half of its travel: and a hand throttle beneath the steering wheel.

The Motor   December 19, 1951.

The Ford Model T - - - - Contd.

inter-connected to this pedal via a simple cam mechanism, so that putting the hand-brake half-on depresses the left-hand pedal to the "neutral" setting, further brake lever movement leaving the engine de-clutched and applying the internal expanding rear wheel brakes. As the gears are engaged by friction clutch and brake band mechanisms, clashing of the gears is impossible.

To drive away, then, the routine is to open the throttle with the fingertips of the left hand, depress the left pedal to engage low gear, and simultaneously release the hand brake with the right hand. When the car is well under way, the low gear pedal can be released gently, the throttle being simultaneously eased back to smooth out the engagement of high gear. With high gear engaged, the driver's feet take no further part in the control of car speed until braking is required, the speed control being the hand throttle set conveniently by the driver's left finger tips. The ignition control set conveniently at the driver's right hand also needs adjustment, mainly in accordance with speed but also to a less extent in relation to throttle opening, to maintain smooth, vigorous and economical engine operation without knocking. Getting the best out of the engine is obviously something of an art, although quite a small amount of experience will allow an intelligent driver to obtain results which, will at least be very good.

Brisk Acceleration

The combination of generous engine size with low car weight results in very lively performance, and the Ford is no sluggard in modern town traffic. As the acceleration figures published on the data page show, there is very brisk acceleration up to 35 m.p.h. available, either from rest through the gears or from 10 m.p.h. in high gear. This figure of 35 m.p.h. may be regarded as the car's comfortable main road cruising speed, the wind resistance of a really ample windscreen combining with the throttling effect of a small-bore carburetter to cut down the maximum speed to little more than 40 m.p.h.

The riding comfort provided by the undamped springs is quite reasonable on present-day roads, light axles and a notably well upholstered non-adjustable seat helping very considerably : such slight pitching as does occur is felt mainly as fore-and-aft motion, in consequence of

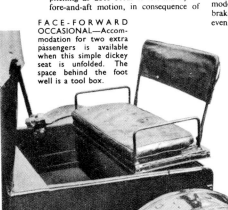

FACE-FORWARD OCCASIONAL—Accommodation for two extra passengers is available when this simple dickey seat is unfolded. The space behind the foot well is a tool box.

a high seating position on a short chassis. The test car steered very satisfactorily, the high geared steering (with an extremely compact turning circle) being free from lost motion, but corners required to be treated with some respect as the high-pressure tyres seemed more liable to hop on bumps or to slide on wet surfaces than are present-day varieties.

The two-seater body on the test car, although the least expensive in the Ford range, was extremely comfortable, its height in conjunction with the shortness of the bonnet providing truly magnificent all-round vision. Entry to the body is very easy through the near side door, but less so through the opposite door owing to the positioning of the handbrake and the fairing around the steering column and control rods. A dickey seat able to seat two extra passengers can be unfolded, and behind this there is an accessible tool locker. Erection of the hood was extremely quick and simple, with two people working, but the absence of a wiper on the easily-folded windscreen made wet-weather driving somewhat unpleasant. The headlamps on the test car had not been linked up to the acetylene gas generator, and a youth of the electronic age had filled the oil-burning side and tail lamps with lubricating oil instead of paraffin, so we can say little about night driving qualities except that a high seating position almost eliminates dazzle from following cars.

Braking is the respect in which the model T falls seriously short of 1951 standards, and it is unwise to follow too closely behind other vehicles. With moderate pressure, however, the foot brake will give a fairly quick stop and will even lock the rear wheels—as it is a transmission brake, running in oil, it is advisable to release it at intervals on long descents to ensure that the lining does not become dry. The retarding effect of the engine operates only slowly when the throttle is closed, but engagement of low gear (a matter simply of pressing the left-hand pedal) provides a strong retarding action. For a driver accustomed to other cars, it is necessary to remember that, with this Ford epicyclic transmission,

stopping the car without stalling the engine involves finally obtaining neutral : this can be done either by *half* depressing the left hand pedal (fully depressing it engages low gear) or by half applying the handbrake, full application of this before the car has stopped being inadvisable.

Manœuvres in confined spaces are easy once the proper technique is learned : it is simply a case of releasing the handbrake to the half-on position with the right hand, opening the throttle with the left hand, and gradually depressing either the left hand or the central pedal to produce either forward or reverse motion at a low speed. The ratios of low and reverse gears are such that no high speeds can be attained in them without considerable engine fuss—steering in reverse requires care, due to reversal of the vigorous self-centring castor action.

The Maintenance Aspect

Some reference must be made to the question of maintenance work, to amplify the customary details tabulated on our data page. In one respect, maintenance work on this car is easier than on modern cars, because almost every component is of simple design, because the whole mechanism is not enclosed within easy-to-clean but hard-to-remove sheet metal, and because the floorboards can be removed and replaced in a very few seconds. The number of mechanical details requiring daily attention is, however, very much greater than in these days of rubber or self-lubricating bushes, and it must be recalled that a roadside puncture involves replacing an inner tube in a non-detachable wheel.

Driving this 1912 Ford, and knowing how fundamentally reliable the model T proved, we realized once again what a real need it must have filled during the first quarter of the 20th century. Simple and inexpensive, with good power for acceleration and hill climbing but a modest maximum speed, and able not merely to go anywhere but also to be kept serviceable with sketchy workshop facilities, it is the sort of vehicle the re-appearance of which in modern guise might prove widely popular in this hard-up third quarter of the century.

AMPLE HEADROOM—Ease of entry to the comfortable two-seater body is not impaired when the easy-to-erect hood is raised. The windscreen is very effective, but the hood produces an appreciable amount of back-draught.

Owner's View

*Michael Allen talks to Bob and
Les Croft. Between them, the Croft
family own six Model Ts,
including the green 1915 Tourer
and the 1922 Speedster featured
in this book. Les Croft also serves
as Vice-President of the Model T
Register of Great Britain.*

M.A. Why are you so interested in
the Model T.?
B. & L.C. We're Ford mad. We've
always used Fords so when we
wanted to get into the vintage car
scene it obviously had to be
Model Ts.
M.A. I'm extremely impressed by
your beautiful 1915 Tourer. When
did you acquire this, and what sort
of condition was it in then?
B. & L.C. It was some years ago;
we found it in a barn. Actually, it
was running but very rough, and
the bodywork was in pieces.
M.A. Were there any problems
restoring it to such a high
standard?
B. & L.C. No, we did very well
through the Model T Register from
which, as you know, you can get
all the parts. We had all the wood
treated against woodworm,
although, in fact, the wood wasn't
actually too bad. The entire

metalwork was stripped bare and
treated with a de-rusting solution
as the intitial preparation before
painting. The seats were covered
in sacking, with the original
upholstery being almost
non-existent. A local upholsterer,
John Ham, re-covered the seats,
and we're very pleased with the
result.
M.A. What advice would you give
someone else facing similar work?
B. & L.C. Have a lot of patience; if
you have then it's very enjoyable
really to see the car gradually
being restored.
M.A. In our run today I was
frankly amazed by how well the
Tourer coped with both the traffic
in town and then got along so
well on the open road; how do
you rate its performance and
handling?
B. & L.C. Terrific for its year, it
really must have been fantastic in
its time. It can take Buckhaw
Brow (a notorious local hill) in
top – just – but it will do it! We've
got harder linings (from Mintex)
on the transmission brake band
now, but it's still exciting in hilly
country with only transmission
and rear wheel brakes, you do
have to judge early for braking.
Handling doesn't give any
problems within its performance
range really.
M.A. Are any of your Model Ts in
what you could call regular use?
B. & L.C. Oh yes, every week
during the summer. I *(Bob)* use
this one (the green Tourer) for
business at times, visiting
wholesalers in the district. I came
out of one place recently when it
had started to rain suddenly, and
had to ask for some help with
putting up the hood. When he
came out the fellow said: ''You're
not going home in that are you?
Its got no windscreen wipers!''.
We've done some miles in it, it's
so reliable. Obviously, it's a bit
limited, because you can't really
leave it around just anywhere.
I *(Les)* used our other Tourer to
go on holiday to Hastings last year
(from Morecambe), it was a really

enjoyable week, no problems. It's
got to be the most reliable of all
the veteran/vintage cars. *(Bob)*
Oh yes, on the veteran car runs
you know, it's always the others
that break down, not the Fords.
M.A. Has the green Tourer won
any concours awards?
B. & L.C. Yes, last year it won the
Blackpool-Morecambe Rally.
M.A. I know you have been
actively involved in the owners'
club yourselves for some time
now, how helpful is membership
for the Model T owner?
B. & L.C. It's vital really, from the
spares point of view alone. It's
also a very friendly outfit, with a
really nice crowd of people.
M.A. Do they have any major
meetings?
B. & L.C. Yes, and we go to many
meetings, including the really long
distance ones.
M.A. How would you both sum
up the enjoyment you get from
your Model T Fords?
B. & L.C. (Bob) No safety belts
needed! *(Les)* It's so different from
modern motoring. It calms you
down after the modern pace of
things, and it's surprising how
friendly people are towards you;
you enjoy talking to them and
telling them all about the cars.
M.A. Obviously, Model Ts are not
widely available for sale, so what
advice would you give to a
potential owner?
B. & L.C. Well, they do become
available amongst the club
membership, so it may well pay to
enquire there first.

*Michael Allen interviews Tony
Chesters, whose Model T
collection consisting of a 1915
Tourer, 1920 centre-door Sedan,
and 1923 Australian Tourer also
appear in this book.*

M.A. Why are you so interested in
the Model T?
T.C. I've always had an interest in
old vehicles, and I first bought a
Model TT truck in 1974 and the
interest just grew from there; I
then bought the Sedan in 1975.

M.A. The Sedan is obviously in fine condition now, but what was it like when you bought it?

T.C. Rather roughly painted, but otherwise very original. Quite good mechanically, too, although it has had the valves and big-ends done since, but nothing drastic.

M.A. Were there any problems with getting parts?

T.C. No, the club is very active, you can get all the spares now.

M.A. Would it have been more economical to have purchased one not even needing that small amount of work?

T.C. You probably wouldn't have been able to find one, so I don't think it would really.

M.A. How do you rate Model T performance and handling?

T.C. The Sedan is not quite so good as the Tourer in respect of performance because of its greater weight. The maximum speed is about the same but the acceleration is down slightly. It rolls rather more on corners too because of the greater top end weight of the body, although it's just as comfortable as the Tourer.

M.A. Are any of your Model Ts in regular use?

T.C. Yes, we've been on holiday in the Sedan.

M.A. How practical are they for regular use in your opinion?

T.C. I find the Sedan more practical than the earlier Tourer as it has the later electric lighting. As a practical usable car you can't find anything better of that age than a Model T. People were reluctant to use them a few years ago when they couldn't always get the bits to maintain and repair them, but that's changed now and there are a lot of members who use them.

M.A. Would you consider the running cost high for a Model T today?

T.C. No, not really, spares are very reasonably priced from the Register, although tyres are perhaps expensive. My Sedan does about 27mpg, and the insurance costs are not high either.

M.A. Have any of your cars won any prizes in concours events?

T.C. Oh yes, too numerous to list really. They tend to be judged on originality and the Sedan usually gets an award wherever it is entered.

M.A. How would you sum up the enjoyment you get from owning your Model Ts?

T.C. By the fact that I've got three and you can see what condition they are in. The fact also that the family can go to the Register meetings in them as they really are family-orientated rallies. The Model T seems to create a lot more interest generally than do the fancy veteran or vintage cars, and they certainly bring back a lot of memories to people which is what old cars are about to many of them. I've yet to find anything which creates as much interest as these.

M.A. What advice would you give to a potential owner of a Model T?

T.C. Don't be afraid to buy one. The Register will help on any matter, it's a very down-to-earth club and there are always people willing to help you out.

BUYING

Buying

Should he ever look down from upon high, Henry Ford will certainly be pleased to see that his beloved Tin Lizzie is alive and well, and, appropriately, completely outnumbering her surviving contemporaries with an estimated 100,000 examples worldwide, of which half are in her native America. It would please him just as much also to see the active owners' clubs and their superb spares back-up which ensures that in the United States and Britain in particular, the Model T owner today is secure in the knowledge that any spare part required is readily available. Also in typical Ford fashion, Model T prices, whilst naturally reflecting condition amongst themselves, are generally less than one would expect to pay for another make car of similar age. Thus, the easiest way for the enthusiast to enjoy some motoring in the style of 70 years or so ago is to acquire a Model T Ford and become a member of the appropriate club.

In fact, it may well prove advantageous to someone committed to the purchase of a Model T to take out club membership first; this could assist greatly in the search for a suitable car as the clubs usually know of just what is, or could well be, available for purchase. Membership will also allow the future owner the opportunity of becoming acquainted with good examples of the model, therefore helping considerably in the future assessment of a particular car.

Which model?

Without doubt the most usable of what are nowadays loosely termed 'veteran' cars, the Model T Ford is quite capable of covering long distances to rallies etc., and, incredible though it may seem to the casual observer, in several cases today there are examples which still go some way towards actually earning their keep from time-to-time by being used occasionally for more normal business by their owners. Bearing this in mind, whilst no doubt contemplating the Model T as an interesting hobby, the buyer should establish at the outset which would be the most suitable variation should the old Ford be pressed into normal service on occasion. The number of passengers in particular, or the desirability of the weather protection afforded by the Sedans, for instance, are factors which perhaps ought to be taken into account as much as whether a brass radiator, or otherwise, is a prime consideration. Although, of course, bearing in mind the variations originally available, finding a very specific example could take considerable time.

Examination

The Model T's simplicity and such good accessiblity are of great value to the prospective purchaser when examining an example being offered for sale. The chassis and running gear can be quite easily inspected due to the very open nature of the construction, with the high ground clearance being of real help if it is felt necessary to crawl underneath the car in order to inspect closely such items as the radius rod attachments etc. The appearance alone of the bodywork and fenders (mudguards) should give a reasonably good indication of their true condition in the case of the metalwork content. The condition of the floorboarding, too, should be easily determined, although accurately assessing the state of the wooden framework will require greater diligence. Overall, however, this very simply constructed vehicle with its pleasing lack of the many mud and water traps of much more recent cars should not hide anything of a very serious nature even from the purchaser who has little knowledge of the model, but who takes time and care over the inspection procedure.

Appreciably more audible in a general sense by comparison with more modern units, the big four-cylinder engine runs quite smoothly within its modest revolution range, and the checks which would be carried out with a modern unit apply equally here. If there are no smoke signals, no obvious knocking noises or rattle, then the engine can almost certainly be assumed to have a useful lease of life ahead of it. On the road, with the ignition system and carburation in good condition, the engine should provide sufficient torque to impart a pleasantly effortless feel to the car's progress, with a quite surprising amount of acceleration available anywhere between around 15mph and 40 to 50mph in high gear. Low gear gives an adequately brisk getaway from rest, and there will be few hills, if any, which a Model T would not climb in this ratio.

If the low gear and reverse gear band linings are in good

condition, taking up the drive in either forward or reverse directions should be almost silky smooth, as will the change into high when the forward gear pedal is released. Skilful use of the hand throttle during moving off and subsequently changing into high does result in quite astonishingly smooth progress with a Model T in fine fettle, and if the vendor can demonstrate this, the prospective purchaser can almost certainly be assured that all is well with the transmission.

The standard chassis able to take each of the many body styles available, and the interchangeability of parts between many model years has made the Model T a relatively easy car to restore, and also to build up from scratch using major items salvaged from the remains of more than one car. Therefore, in view also of the excellent spares availability today, a Model T in need of restoration may well be an attractive proposition to the would-be owner with the time to devote to such a project. When extensive restoration or rebuilding has already taken place on a car up for sale it can result in some difficulty in establishing the particular car's present day authenticity in respect of its

original year of manufacture, so the buyer wishing for absolute accuracy of detail could find the search for a suitable car rather more difficult than if just a nice representative example would suffice. Of course, once a car has been purchased, it need not be an impossible task to locate and acquire replacement parts with which to achieve a greater degree of originality if desired.

Summing up

Overall, a Model T should present no insurmountable problems, and anyone keen to own one need not hesitate to buy if the funds are available for a car which checks out satisfactorily for the price demanded. Club membership would seem to be not just

desirable but absolutely essential in Britain, if for no other reason than to gain access to the spare parts necessary to keep it in good running order. It would be a pity, however, to use the clubs solely for this purpose, as amongst the membership there is a vast fund of knowledge and experience upon which the newcomer is free to draw; knowledge which, coupled with the friendships formed at the social get-togethers and car rallies, can greatly enhance the pleasures of Model T motoring today.

CLUBS, SPECIALISTS & BOOKS

Clubs

Model T Ford Club of America. P.O. Box 7400, Burbank, California 91510/7400 – this club has many chapters throughout the United States, plus three in neighbouring Canada, and one in Great Britain (see below).

Model T Ford Club International. P.O. Box 915, Elgin, Chicago, Illinois 60120.

Antique Auto Club. 501 West Grosvenor Road, Hershey, Pennsylvania 17033.

Model T Ford Register of Great Britain. Secretary, Alan Meakin, 14 Breck Farm Lane, Taverham, Norwich, Norfolk.

Model T Ford Register of Holland. c/o A. Martini, Postbus 2146, 1180 EC Anstelveen, Holland.

Ancient Ford Club of Belgium. 350 Micksebaan, B/2130 Brasschaat, Belgium.

Model T Ford Club of Australia. P.O. 18, Hurstville, N.S.W. 2220.

Ford Model T Register of Australia. P.O. 134, St Marys, S.A. 5042.

Model T Ford Club of Victoria. c/o Dennis Page, 4 Miriam Ct., Templestone, Victoria 3106.

Specialists

A network of Model T spares specialists operates throughout America, giving a complete coverage of the model and so enabling the 50,000 or so Model Ts in America to be maintained in the excellent working order of their early years. Overseas, the spares situation is handled almost entirely by the appropriate owners' clubs, who carry large stocks of parts imported from the United States on a regular basis.

Books

Numerous books dealing exclusively with one or more of the many aspects of the Model T have been published over the years, particularly in its homeland of America. Other general Ford histories, and Henry Ford biographies have also included much information of interest to the Model T enthusiast. Many of these books are now out of print, but nevertheless can often be found on sale amongst the secondhand stock at specialist motoring-book outlets. The following list is a representative selection of what has been and in some cases still is, available:

The Model T Ford: From Here to Obscurity by R. Miller and B. McCally. A large format hardbound book giving an incredibly detailed pictorial history of the Model T throughout its production run. More than 900 photographs of preserved or accurately restored Model Ts on a year-by-year basis. Still in print and widely available.

Down Memory Lane with the Model T by L. Maurer. Includes reminiscences from former Model T owners interviewed by the author.

Ford Model T Scrapbook by F. Clymer. Model T photographs and reproduced period adverts etc.

Floyd Clymer's Model T Memories (Including The Ubiquitous Model T) by L. Henry.

Model T Restoration Handbook by L. Henry. Illustrated guide to restoring the Model T.

The Model T Ford by A. Bird. Profile Publications No. 13, a 10-page booklet giving brief overview of the Model T.

Model T Ford Authentic Accessories Vol. 1 & Vol. 2 by J. Kenealy. Reproductions of period advertisements describing Model T accessories.

Model T Ford Service and Shop Manual Reprint of original Ford factory publication.

Model T Ford Service Bulletin Essentials Reprint of service bulletins issued to Ford dealers.

The Original Book of the Ford by R.T. Nicholson, published by The Motor. An in-depth owners' handbook/manual.

Ford Military Vehicles by L. Geary. Includes specification of Model T ambulances and scout cars. Still in print and widely available.

My Life and Work by Henry Ford in collaboration with Samuel Crowther.

The Triumph of an Idea: The Story of Henry Ford by R. Graves.

The Ford Dynasty by J. Brough.

Ford: The Dust and the Glory, A Racing History by L. Levine.

1

2

PHOTO GALLERY

1. Model T Touring Car, clearly showing the original two-pedal, two-lever control arrangements. The folding top was an extra-cost option on the earliest models.

2. When devoid of even rear passenger doors, the Model Ts were sometimes referred to as 'Tourabouts', or 'Toursters'. The cylindrical object on the running board is the gas generator for the acetylene headlamps.

3. The top, windshield, and headlamps had become standard equipment on the open cars by 1911. It was with this model that Trafford Park went into production in October of that year.

4. The Roadster featured a single seat on the rear deck, with its remoteness from the other two occupants quickly earning it the nickname of the 'mother-in-law' seat. Without this seat, and just a plain rear deck, the open car was known as the Runabout.

3

4

5. The Town Car, with rear passenger division and closed-car amenities was popular with taxi operators, whilst being an ideal chauffeur-driven car, too.

6. A period Ford advertisement depicts the Model T Delivery Car introduced for 1911.

7. By 1913 front doors had appeared on the Touring Car, although that on the driver's side was a fixed dummy fitting, thus forcing the driver to alight on the kerbside.

1911

Demand for Ford Cars Doubles Annually

100,000 Ford Cars Are in Service Now

Ford
Model T Delivery Car

$700

Fully Equipped with Automobile Brass Windshield

Speedometer

Three Oil Lamps

Two Gas Lamps

Generator

Horn

Tools

8

10

9

8. *Another 1913 Touring Car, differing completely from that previously illustrated by virtue of the British designed and built bodywork, which was used early in 1913 apparently because of some difficulty in supplies from America.*

9. & 10. *A recently restored example of the rare 1913 British Model T. This car features the Runabout bodywork to which has been added a neat breadvan rear end.*

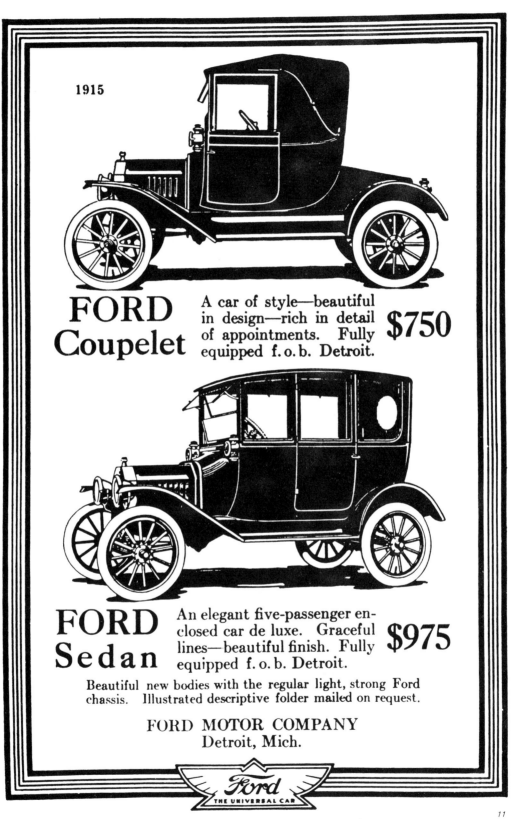

1915

FORD Coupelet

A car of style—beautiful in design—rich in detail of appointments. Fully equipped f. o. b. Detroit.

$750

FORD Sedan

An elegant five-passenger enclosed car de luxe. Graceful lines—beautiful finish. Fully equipped f. o. b. Detroit.

$975

Beautiful new bodies with the regular light, strong Ford chassis. Illustrated descriptive folder mailed on request.

FORD MOTOR COMPANY
Detroit, Mich.

Ford
THE UNIVERSAL CAR

11

11. 1915 saw the introduction of the Coupelet and the Sedan. The louvres in the bonnet (hood) sides, and the curved rear mudguards were also new this year.

13

12. & 13. A beautifully restored 1915 Touring Car
shows off the Model T's frontal and rear aspects. The
slender tyres run at around 55 psi.

14. Like many Model Ts, UY 2125 has acquired a set of
detachable wheels as offered by some accessory
manufacturers, and therefore carries a complete spare
wheel – a big improvement over a puncture outfit!

12

14

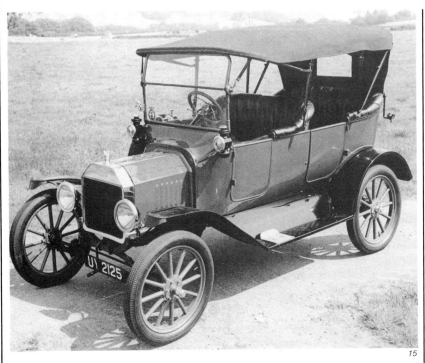

15.

15. The nicely curved cowl and fully curved rear fenders (mudguards) of the 1915 cars were early examples of styling touches incorporated into the Model T for their own sake.

16. The deeply upholstered seats look very inviting, with the fully upholstered side panels giving quite a luxurious appearance which rather belied the Model T's low purchase price.

17. No locks, and just a very simple catch.

18. & 19. With two people on hand, little more than a minute is required in which to raise or lower the top; with only one, however, it's well nigh impossible!

16.

17.

18.

19.

20

21

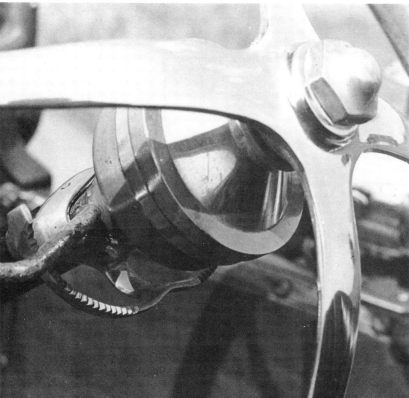

22

20. A neat accessory cover was available for when the top was folded.

21. A brass accessory tread-plate protects the running boards at the much-used front nearside entry/exit point.

22. The hand throttle beneath the steering box, and just visible on the other side the quadrant for the ignition advance/retard lever. Later Model Ts had black-painted steering wheel 'spiders' rather than brass as featured here.

23. Also nicely to hand, the brass Klaxon horn which replaced the rubber bulb variety of the earlier Model Ts.

24. Polished brass, too, for the rearview mirror.

23

24

25

26

27

28

25. & 26. Although electric headlamps appeared in 1915, kerosene side and tail lamps were to remain: the latter featuring a white side lens to illuminate the number plate.

27 & 28. Twisting two O rings and lifting with the handle would release the engine compartment sides. The cylinder head joint can be clearly seen as can the integrally cast cylinders and crankcase upper half.

29. The engine number here indicates that this 1915 Tourer has at some stage been fitted with a replacement engine from a later car.

30. The genuine Ford oilcan is a nice original touch.

29

30

31

32

33

34

35

36

31. Water circulation is by the thermo-siphon principle, with a four-bladed fan driven by a particularly robust-looking fan-belt assisting in the cooling arrangements.

32. The updraught carburettor is situated on the right-hand side of the engine. The forked rod is the mixture control which can be regulated from the driving position; the horizontal rod is the choke control which protrudes out of the front conveniently close to the starting handle.

33. Just a simple loop in the control rod is every bit as effective as a separate knob.

34. Also on the right-hand side is the oil filler tube, conveniently situated at the front where it renders topping up an easy operation. However ...

35. ... no dipstick is provided, and checking the oil level is not nearly so convenient. Two taps at the rear of the flywheel housing are provided for this task. If oil runs out of the top one when opened, the level is too high. If no oil escapes when the lower tap is opened then the level is too low. The correct level is half-way in between, and not surprisingly ...

36. ... the accessory manufacturers were soon offering simple oil-level gauges such as that depicted here attached to the lower tap position.

37

38

37. 38. & 39. Another superb example of the 1915 Touring Car. Although fitted with the later, demountable | *outer wheel rims, EL 1733 carries an interesting accessory spare tyre and rim which can be simply* | *clamped to the outside of the offending wheel and tyre in the event of a puncture.*

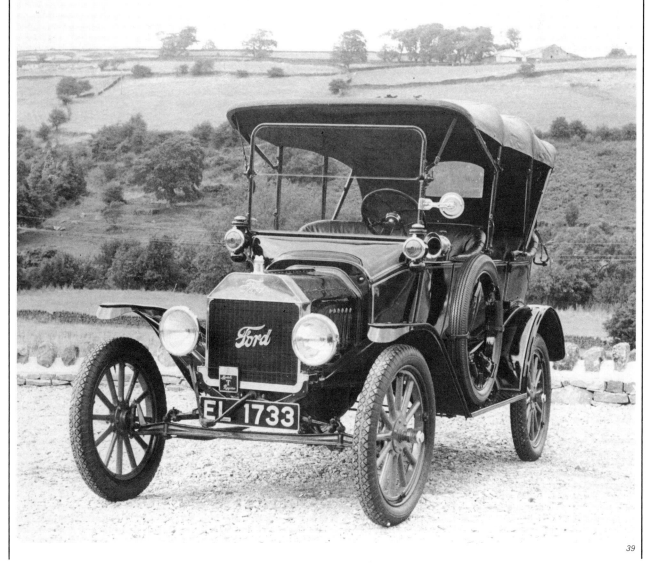

39

40

41

42

43

44

40. Close-up detail of the spare rim clamps.

41. The headlamps came from outside sources, with the maker's name usually appearing in addition to that of Ford. Plain glass lenses did not give way to the patterned variety (which give an improved spread of light) until 1921.

42. The gleaming brass radiator of EL 1733 reveals 'MADE IN U.S.A.' beneath what is surely the most famous piece of script in the entire motoring world. Still in use today, it is instantly recognisable amongst the plethora of often indecipherable 'modern art' logos adorning other makes of car.

43. Four prominent ears assist in removal of the Model T's radiator cap. Not all filler necks were riveted to the header tank as shown here; some were soldered on.

44. The ends of the bolts securing the road spring at its centre attachment point can just be seen either side of the starting handle, which itself is neatly secured by a leather strap. The rather spindly-looking axle, steering rods etc., belie their great strength.

45

45. The appropriate part number, T 202, is embossed on the vanadium steel axle.

46. & 47. Rear end details of EL 1733 reveal that auxiliary coil spring shock absorbers have been fitted at the leaf spring extremities. The double curvature necessary for the main spring to clear the final drive housing can be clearly seen, as can the torque tube enclosing the propeller shaft. The large cylindrical object is the silencer from which emerged a very short tailpipe that ended before the rear of the car.

48. The driving compartment in this case features an authentic Ford rubber mat. The coil box, with ignition key inserted here, is situated on the bulkhead. The foot pedals are from L to R low/high forward gears, reverse gear, and the transmission brake.

49. Rear interior view of EL 1733 shows quite clearly the difference in texture between the leathercloth upholstery and the real leather panel adjacent to the door.

46

47

48

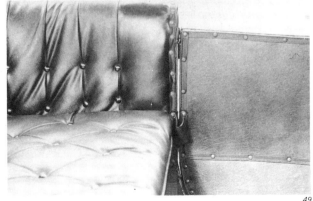

49

50

51

52

50. & 51. With the adoption of the steel radiator the opportunity was taken to redesign the hood (bonnet) so allowing it to fair into the curved cowl. A hand operated windshield wiper and a rearview mirror can be seen in these views of CO 4208 which, apart from a repaint, is an original unrestored example of the centre door Sedan.

52. 53. & 54. The front, side, and rear profile of the Ford Sedan. Apart from the rather small rear window, the glass area was generous.

55. Also running on demountable rims, CO 4208 carries the authentic spare rim and tyre for this arrangement. 30 in. x $3^1/2$ in. tyres all round were used with the demountable rims.

54

53

55

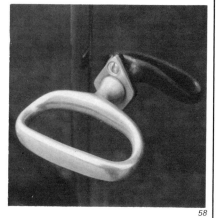

56   57   58

56. The toothed wheel attachment to the front hub indicates that CO 4208 has been equipped with a speedometer at some stage, although the instrument, cable and driven gear don't remain now. Speedometers were standard factory equipment at times during the model's early years, and were widely available from accessory manufacturers.

57. A lovely period piece adorning this Model T's running board is the Shell spare petrol can with separate compartment (cap removed here) for spare engine oil.

58. Along with the headlamp rims, the door handles also featured a nickel finish which relieved the expanse of black. A rather less attractive T handle was a feature of some Sedans.

59. 60. & 61. Closed comfort. Roomy, yet somehow quite cosy, the 1920 Sedan interior still has something of a carriage 'air' about it. The window blinds and strap-type window opening arrangements are in sharp contrast to today's cars – as is the quite enormous amount of headroom! The rear seat view reveals that the 66 year old upholstery in this remarkably original car is at last beginning to show its age.

59

60   61

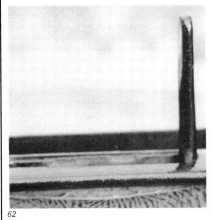

62

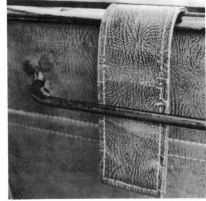

63

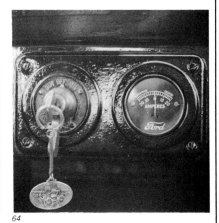

64

65

62. & 63. As on the Tourer, just a simple door release mechanism was provided on the Sedan, with a separate, conveniently long door-pull for closing the doors from inside.

64. An ammeter made its appearance with the battery and generator-equipped cars, whilst the ignition key vacated its former position in the coil box for a new home in a combined ignition/lighting switch.

65. Long before the days of plastic window stickers, engraved metal plates were used by motor car agencies to advertise their services. One wonders whether H. Andrew & Co. Ltd., of Plymouth, would ever have guessed that this plate would still be proclaiming their business 60 years or so on!

66. Another steel radiatored Model T which, judging by the front seat, apparently started life as either a Runabout, or Touring Car. The rear bodywork is thought to be a one-off job carried out as recently as the late 1940s. The mudguards do not seem to match those of any production Model T, and this fact, coupled with the lack of side valances above the running boards, suggests that perhaps the originals were in a poor state when this Model T was converted.

67. The lack of valances reveals the longitudinal chassis members ...

66

67

68. & 69. ... and such details as the handbrake operating rods and rear radius arms.

70. & 71. The interior views of ST 2614 show the characteristic front seat of the open Model Ts, along with a really useful passenger carrying capacity in the rear. The tubular steel uprights support a fabric-covered roof of wooden construction.

72. 73. & 74. Another, rather more drastic, conversion has been carried out on this 1922 Model T, resulting in a 'speedster' of the type so popular in the 1920s. The raised front wheel spindles, and lowered outer spring mountings, which together result in a much lower car overall, can be clearly seen. The rear view shows the fuel tank which has been repositioned behind, rather than under, the front seat as in the normal Model T, whilst the Touring Car also featured in this view serves to emphasize the speedster's low stance.

68

69

70

71

72

73

74

75

75. A genuine Ford accessory water temperature gauge adorns the radiator of WFX 280. The winged radiator cap is one of several alternative designs, and suits the speedster very well.

76. An SU carburettor is one of the visible indications of WFX 280's modified engine, on which a coil and distributor ignition system replaces the flywheel magneto. A raised compression ratio cylinder head (modified Ford) and lightweight aluminium pistons are further aids to an improved power output. A rear axle ratio of 3.1 : 1 has replaced the normal 3.64 : 1 final drive set up. All of this has endowed WFX 280 with a 60 mph capability – authenticated by police radar! (Not, is must be added, that the speedster was breaking the law; the occasion, in fact, being a demonstration run.)

77. The ultimate Model T speedster's powerplants were those equipped with the Frontenac O.H.V. cylinder heads and multiple carburettor installations. The example of such an engine shown here is on display in the Henry Ford Museum, and is interesting also in that it shows the Model T's extremely compact gearbox.

78. & 79. In sharp contrast to the speedster bodies available is this interesting proprietary conversion, the

76

77

78

79

Mifflinburg 'Suburban' body which resulted in a very useful short wheelbase bus. A 1923 example, ER 7449, features the later headlamps with patterned glass.

80. & 81. The interior details reveal six passenger accommodation plus the driver. Complete weather protection is afforded by the roll-down side curtains which include a generous window area.

80

81

82

83

82. The underside of ER 7449 clearly shows the combined lower half of the crankcase and flywheel housing. Troughs in the detachable bottom panel ensure the crankshaft big ends pick up oil on every revolution. The front axle's radius rods have their rear mounting point situated on the front of the flywheel cover. In this view the vehicle is on front axle stands, with the front wheel having been detached for some attention and seen here simply leaning against the car.

83. Later in 1923 a restyling of the engine compartment and cowl resulted in a cleaner overall appearance. A neat panel was also introduced to cover the area immediately below the radiator. This 1923 Touring Car is interesting in that it was assembled in Australia from parts supplied by Ford of Canada and is unusual in that it features a brass radiator, windscreen frame and headlamp rims at a time when these were normally painted metal.

84. With just a tonneau cover, and the 1923-style raked-back windshield, DS 7086 has quite a racy look about it.

84

85

86

88

85. & 86. The availability of the Ford 1 ton truck chassis broadened the Model T's appeal considerably. This particular example was assembled at Ford's Bordeaux plant in 1925, and is believed to have given some 40 years of service as a vineyard truck. The open front at each side of the loading area allowed the carriage of the long canes used in the vineyard. The close-up view shows uprated front suspension with additional transverse leaf spring.

87. XD 8457 boasts full electrical equipment, with the dynamo situated on the front right, from where it is driven by the camshaft gears. The starter motor is on the left-hand side, and with this equipment the choke control is re-routed to the driving compartment.

88. With the seat and floorboards removed the transmission is revealed, with the normal two-speed epicyclic gearbox seen here on the right of the picture. A proprietary lever-operated auxiliary gearbox has been fitted in this case, giving XD 8457 a total of four forward speeds. Immediately behind this can be seen the underseat transverse fuel tank.

89. The overhead worm drive rear axle was a feature of the 1 ton truck chassis only. Also visible here is the smaller diameter rear wheel and larger tyre with which most of the late model trucks appear to have been equipped.

87

89

The Model T in its Final Stage

AUGUST, 1927

| TWO-SEATER £120 |  |  | LIGHT VAN £122 |

| TOURING CAR £125 |  |  | ENCLOSED LIGHT VAN £140 |

| COUPE £170 |  |  | TON TRUCK £137 |

| TUDOR SALOON £190 |  |  | TON VAN £142 |

| FORDOR SALOON £215 |  |  | ENCLOSED TON VAN £190 |

90. The final line-up of Model T Fords available in Britain in the summer of 1927 when production ceased.

91. (This page and over). A selection of the range of accessories and equipment that became available for the Model T from outside sources, and which eventually numbered more than 5000 items.

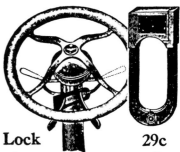
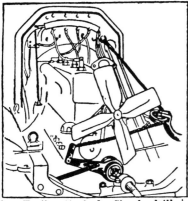